CRE

REST

ENTERING THE LORD'S REST AMIDST LIFE'S JOURNEY

Elizabeth Zacharias

Created to Rest: Entering the Rest of the Lord Amidst Life's Journey

© Copyright 2019--**Elizabeth Zacharias**

Cover design by Pixelstudio

Cover photo from Istock

ACKNOWLEDGMENTS

I want to thank my wonderful husband, Dan, and my oldest daughter, Moriah, for their support and their help with proofreading and editing.

I would also like to thank my good friend, Jackie Mcgirven-Maresco, for her assistance in editing. Christianbookdoctor.com

Many thanks also go to my friend, Beth Jones, who encouraged and coached me all along the way.

TABLE OF CONTENTS

INTRODUCTION

Have you ever wondered what it means to enter the rest of the Lord? It sounds somewhat mystical and beyond our understanding. How can we as human beings with bodies of flesh, enter into something that seems contrary to the active lifestyles we often live?

My husband Dan has been trying to get a handle on this issue for over 30 years. Until recently, I saw it more as "his thing." But to my surprise, the Lord has also begun speaking to me about it. The longer I thought about it, the more I realized that the Lord has been dealing with me in this area most of my life. I came to the conclusion that if He has been trying to get both my husband's and my attention on the topic of rest, then it is very likely that God desires to convey this experience to others.

I've pondered this topic over the past several years. How can we have that rest which the Lord promised the Israelites (Exodus 22:17) in such an active form? It seems to be a paradox. And why do the New Testament Scriptures talk about entering rest anyways? Sometimes finding the answers have seemed impossible.

I wondered what it would take for someone to enter God's rest. So few people   that I know, claim to possess it. One person I knew who came close to doing so was an elderly woman that was a family friend. She never actually spoke about the rest of the Lord. She exemplified it.

This woman was one of my grandmother's best friends. We knew her as Aunt Jenny. We all lived on a quiet country road which meandered close to a tidal river along the coast of Maine in the town of Ellsworth. Everyone on the road knew each other and it was not uncommon for us to offer help to those who needed it. My grandmother lived next door to us and Aunt Jenny lived less than a quarter of a mile down the road. Aunt Jenny or Jenny Patten, as most people knew her, had lived there most of her life and had received Jesus as her Savior in the late 1930's.

Her house was a fairly small white farmhouse with forest green trim. I remember the scent of the beach roses soothed me as I walked past the bushes by the road. I'd continue   to the white hydrangea tree in the front yard. When I arrived on her large front porch there were several hand caned rocking chairs tempting visitors to sit.

Entering her house was like stepping back in time. The smell of wood smoke greeted me as I stepped over the door sill. An old stand up piano graced the front dining room where my brothers and I used to play "Chopsticks." A crackling fire blazed in a fireplace in the small, narrow parlor of a living room. But most of the smell of smoke came from the antique cast iron wood stove that filled most of her humble kitchen. Aunt Jenny did all her cooking in and on that stove.

Aunt Jenny had hosted a rural Sunday School in her house from the 1940's to the 1980's through an organization called The American Sunday School Union, later known as the American Missionary Fellowship. I remember sitting at the kitchen table in that room, teaching some of my cousins a preschool Sunday School lesson.

Aunt Jenny was a petite, quiet woman with short, snow white hair. She never yelled or shouted when I saw her but she captured our attention and love by her sweet, gentle spirit. She didn't have an easy life either. In her later years, she had a type of blood disorder which made her weak and frail. She didn't have many material possessions, yet she seemed to lack nothing. Her husband, Paul, worked for some people on Cranberry Island in Frenchman's Bay as captain of their boat. Aunt Jenny and her husband were always giving to others. Yet, it was her quiet, restful spirit which I remember most.

She didn't complain about her problems, but often gave out of her own need to those around her. Every Christmas, she and her husband gave my family a handmade newly caned chair or rocking chair and a homemade quilt with all of our names embroidered on it, including our pets. This was greatly appreciated as my family did not have much as far as material possessions were concerned.

Aunt Jenny's quiet spirit spoke volumes, more than any words could have. She lived her life in such a way that showed Christ in her actions. Remembering her gave me courage to move forward in my own quest of entering the rest of the Lord. I could almost see her peering over the balcony of Heaven, cheering me on.

I began to search the scriptures. It started in earnest when I studied the book of Hebrews, reading it through several times in one year. I had previously thought that I knew the book well. But it was amazing how the book opened up to me as I read it over and over again. I received revelations as I continued reading and eagerly looked forward to the time when I could immerse myself in the book, meditating on the words that seemed to have a life of their own. The study moved me forward in my quest for more knowledge of how to enter the rest of the Lord.

This book chronicles my journey through the scriptures and shares my own experiences of how I realized that God has actually created us to enter His rest, what the Lord's rest is and how to maintain it. I also learned that as we journey into God's rest we come to realize that He is our source of rest.

I hope that through reading this book, you are spurred on in your own faith journey into the Lord's rest. And I hope that you come into all that He created you for so that you can receive all His benefits and be transformed into the image of His Son.

MY EXPERIENCE

When I think of rest, I often picture myself at a beautiful lake in the mountains with the call of the loon in the background. The clear crystal water reflects the overhanging trees and mountains as I gaze over the lake. But life seldom allows for us to relocate to such a place or find the time for such an endeavor.

There is a song called "The Times They Are A Changin'" by Bob Dylan and indeed, the times which we live in are rapidly changing. Even a little change can be unsettling, but in these days with wars, rumors of wars, natural disasters, lawlessness and even terrorism, things can seem frightening and out of control.

As a mother of two young adult daughters, I am faced with this issue. I see an uncertain future on the horizon for my husband and I, but especially for my daughters as they start their own lives. Do I face the future with its foreseeable and unforeseeable problems with fear or can I find a better way to deal with these things? Sometimes these questions seem more than I can bear. But I am convinced that there is a better way and I say that from experience.

I remember two incidents where I found myself in dangerous situations. I could have come to harm or even died. Instead, I found myself in a state of peace, which only the Lord could have given me.

My mind was at *rest* the whole time. How did this happen? I believe that in both cases, I found myself in the rest of the Lord.

The most recent incident happened at what was supposed to be a happy event. A friend of ours, Jim, invited Dan and me to Linda's, his wife's, surprise 70th birthday and retirement party. Linda was finally retiring from her insurance job of over 30 years. She had been out with her adult grandson and returned home to a houseful of well-wishers. Over the next few hours, visitors and family enjoyed the food, cake and conversation. The party was a success. Linda beamed. It was evident that she was having a great time.

Now, my husband is a talker. He loves to share about his many adventures. That being the case, we are often among the last to leave a gathering. This time was no different. Dan was in the kitchen talking to some other guests and I was sitting in the front living room opposite Jim and Linda. They were on a sofa facing the picture window. We were in the middle of a conversation when we heard a loud noise coming from the street.

Jim looked out the large picture window. Then he jumped up and yelled, "Liz, you need to move." As I hesitated, he added, "There's a car coming straight at us!" Surprisingly, I wasn't afraid. I had a sense that I wasn't going to be hurt. In what seemed like slow motion, I moved toward the dining room.

About the same time a loud bang shook the front of the house by the picture window.

A small, white truck barreled into the wall underneath the front window, pushing in the bricks beneath it. The car had come across the yard, just missing the large oak trees. None of the little panes were broken in the picture window. Linda was in more shock than I was. She had seen the truck coming right for us, whereas, I had only heard it.

Immediately, Linda's adult son and one of our other friends ran outside to deal with the situation. A woman fell out of the truck, half dazed. "My brakes," she moaned, "They didn't work!" She plopped herself down in the middle of the lawn and made a phone call. It was evident to the two men that she was high on some drug.

I wasn't hurt. The chair that I had been sitting in was not touched either. The only damage to the interior was where some bricks had been pushed in and scraped against the table's leg close to where I'd been sitting. The beautiful stained glass lamp on the table was unscathed.

I had no fear during the entire situation, before, during, or after. I had calmly moved from the chair by the window to another one beside the dining room table. I could have been hurt by the car but somehow in the midst of everything, I knew that I would be safe.

The other situation occurred when I was ten. It was a beautiful day for a picnic. My mother took my siblings and me, along with a group of children from the Sunday school class which she taught, to an outing at a local park on an ocean beach. It was sunny with a refreshing breeze blowing off the water.

That previous spring I had worked hard, saving all my change to buy an inflatable raft. I was anxious to take my raft on the water. But my mother insisted that I let my younger brothers use it first. I was the oldest of four, and I often had to share my toys with my siblings. I remember waiting, rather impatiently, as Mark, age five, played with it near the shore, followed by James, age nine.

Finally, it was my turn. I basked in the sun while the raft floated almost melodically over the water. I was not going to jump on and off the raft which I had seen my younger brothers do. I closed my eyes and sighed. I was enjoying the sun and the water. *All my work had been worth it*! I let my arms dangle over the raft into the cool water. *This is heavenly.* The breeze was blowing just a little, whisking the heat from the sun off of my back. I was at peace.

It seemed like only a moment had gone by when I heard a voice yelling, "Hey, hey you on the raft, the tide is going out." *Why are they calling me?* I wondered. When I looked up, this person appeared to be very, very small. Then he ran into the water, waving his arms. "Don't get off the raft!" he yelled.

I noticed he was up to his waist in water and looked like nothing more than an ant.

Looking around, I saw that I was still in the small cove of the public beach but I had drifted a good ways out with the tide. At that moment, I don't know what kept me from getting off the raft. I just stayed on. I peered down into the depths. Dark black water greeted me. I couldn't imagine how deep it was.

It had only been a few short weeks before that I had made a public confession of my faith in Christ by getting baptized. Both my mother and I had been baptized at the same service. I remembered that as I lay on the raft. Music had played in the background as my mother and I climbed the stairs to the baptismal pool. Then, I was walking into the cool water and being immersed by our pastor. I could feel the coolness, not unlike the water below me. Now, I was floating upon the sea, looking down into it.

I glanced up again towards the miniature beach with all the tiny people. The person who had called out to me was now wildly gesturing and yelling, "Move your arms and swim to shore." I was not a very athletic kid, nor was I a good swimmer. I tried yet it was to no avail. My feeble attempt at paddling didn't seem to get me anywhere.

A sense of peace came over me as I lay on the raft. For some reason, I wasn't afraid. I knew that Jesus loved me and would take care of me. So I started talking to Jesus while I lay there, telling Him that I loved Him. The tide was still going out but I had a sense of peace that I was going to be all right.

I looked back at the beach again. By this time, everyone on the beach was aware of my dilemma. Unbeknownst to me, my grandmother had called Tom, a friend who lived nearby who owned a large row boat, also called a longboat. In no time, they were backing the boat down the ramp and into water. Tom rowed tirelessly, narrowing the distance between us. Soon, he pulled up beside me and hauled me into the longboat, along with my raft. Was I ever glad to be in that boat!

On shore, everyone crowded around me. They were all concerned. "Are you okay?" one asked. Someone threw a blanket across my shoulders. "There, there, you'll be fine now," he said. They were all relieved that I hadn't gotten off the raft. At that point, I wanted to be invisible. True, I was glad that I was on shore and that Tom had come out to get me. But I hadn't felt that I was in any real danger. It had been like I was resting in the arms of Jesus, while I was out on the water.

Even though, I was just a child and a fairly new believer, I knew that the safest place that I could be was resting in Jesus. He was my resting place and my refuge.

> *"I will say of the Lord, He is my refuge and my fortress, My God, in Him, I will trust". (Psalm 91:2)*

At that young age I hadn't yet explored the scriptures and seen how they confirmed my experience. Years later and after much studying on this topic, I know what it represented in my life. It gave me a strong sense of the foundation of the rest of the Lord.

WHAT IS REST?

So what is rest? We usually define rest as a time when you take a break to regain strength. In fact, the Merriam-Webster Dictionary lists three definitions for rest. The first is "reprises sleep; specifically, a bodily state characterized by minimal functional and metabolic activities." The second definition states that it is "(a.) freedom from activity or labor. (b.) a state of motionlessness or inactivity. And (c.) the repose of death." The third definition is "a place for resting or lodging."[i]

When we talk about entering the rest of the Lord, we usually think it refers to the first part of the second definition where it states that it is "a freedom from activity or labor." Is it our freedom or is it the Lord's? I would daresay that it is referring to both. Somehow, when we enter God's "freedom from activity," we have to move into our own "freedom from activity." A.W. Tozer said, "The rest of the Christian is based upon the work of another. It is not his own work for that he could never do. It is done by another who is capable of earning that rest, procuring it. The Christian isn't capable. Nobody is capable."[ii]

If we want to learn how to rest, maybe we should look at God's example. But how does God rest? We get our first glimpse of this in the story of creation in Genesis. God created the heavens, the earth and all that is within it, in six days. He saw it and called it good. Then on the seventh day, He rested (Genesis 2:2). But is resting from work the only rest to which we are invited? I think not. If that were the case, we would still be in the stone-age and not have made the tremendous advances of our own day and age. The Jews of the Old Testament were invited to enter a part of that rest when they were commanded to remember the Sabbath day in Exodus 20:8-11:

"Remember the Sabbath day by keeping it holy. Six days you shall labor and do all your work, but the seventh day is a Sabbath to the Lord your God. On it you shall not do any work, neither you, nor your son or your daughter, nor your male or female servant, nor your animals, nor any foreigner residing in your towns. For in six days the Lord made the heavens and the earth, the sea and all that is in them, but He rested on the seventh day.Therefore the Lord blessed the Sabbath day and made it holy."

So does the word *Sabbath* mean rest from work? Bible Study tools.com says "the origin of the Hebrew Shabbat is uncertain, but it seems to have been derived from the verb *sabat*, meaning to stop, to cease, or to keep. This meaning is rooted in God's rest following the days of creation. (Genesis 2:2-3).[iii]

The Jews were commanded to celebrate the Sabbath and not work on the seventh day of the week. Thus they shared in and remembered God's rest from creation. In this way, they were called to somehow physically partner with God in His rest.

Today, we find this still being played out among Orthodox Jews around the world. On Fridays, you will find them getting all their food ready for the Sabbath day as they are not allowed to cook or even to drive a car. In Israel, the whole nation shuts down except for a few secular Jews and for the many Arabs who live there. In some Jewish communities around the world, there are walking paths around the synagogue neighborhoods called *eruvs* where Orthodox Jews are allowed to walk a short distance on the Sabbath.[iv]   There are strict rules about what can and cannot be done on the Sabbath.

But for the Christian do those rules apply? 1 Corinthians 10:31-33 states,

> *"Therefore, whether you eat or drink, or whatever you do, do all to the glory of God . Give no offense, either to the Jews or to the Greeks or to the church of God, just as I also please all men in all things, not seeking my own profit, but the profit of many, that they may be saved."*

I believe this decision is up to each separate believer to be determined in their own relationship with the Lord. Some Christians feel that they cannot physically work on Saturday. Others have made Sunday as their Sabbath day of rest. A well documented case of this was Eric Liddell, an

Olympic runner who refused to run in the 100 meters qualifying heats in the 1924 summer Olympics because they were on a Sunday. The 1981 movie, Chariots of Fire, was created about this real life story which took place 1924 at the summer Olympics in Paris. He went on to race in the 400 meter race which was scheduled on a weekday and won a gold medal.

Many people today in the Christian church see their Sabbath as being on a Sunday like Eric Liddell did. However, many Messianic Christians still see Saturday as the proper day to have their Sabbath. Others like my husband have jobs which often land on both Saturday or Sunday. My husband has decided to take one day off a week as his Sabbath rest. His schedule is such that his work can fall on any of the week and often changes from week to week. He will have two or three days off each week depending on which shifts he works. He will take one of these days off each week to do nothing more than relax and spend time with the Lord in his personal quiet time. In this way, he ends up being physically refreshed and ready to face the new challenges of the week ahead. He often finds that by giving the day to the Lord, that his other days will go smoother for him, accomplishing more than he had anticipated. In particular, I remember one day that he had taken a "Sabbath rest." Particular tasks came to mind afterwards like cleaning out the gutters where he was able to do the task without any complications and then go on to another task which came to his mind upon completion of the first task. By the end of the day, he had successfully completed a number of different jobs around the house.

It is important to take time to physically rest from your work. During the time of the early pioneers when people were travelling across the country on The Oregon Trail, some of the pioneers thought that they might make better time if they didn't take a day to rest. So some of them went ahead when the group stopped to rest on what was probably a Sunday. Weeks later, the team who had been taking a day off passed the others in the wilderness. The animals and people who had gone ahead were exhausted and their wagons had broken down from disrepair.   So, it is with our lives today, if we do not slow down and take time to rest, we become over exhausted and often broken down.

I find that for myself, as a mother and wife, taking a day off from my responsibilities seems almost impossible but if I take some time in the morning in a quiet place to refresh myself with prayer and by reading from the Bible, I find that I have more energy to face the day ahead.   I can better plan out my day and come at it from a place of inner peace. There is more to entering the rest of the Lord than just resting on the Sabbath. However, it is important to take a day to rest to physically energize oneself for the days ahead.

REST FOR THE SOUL

The New Testament also speaks about rest in Matthew 11:28-30 when Jesus talks to His disciples about finding rest for their souls

> *"Come to Me, all you who labor and are heavy laden, and I will give you rest. Take my yoke upon you and learn from Me, for I am gentle And lowly in heart and you will find rest for your souls, For My yoke is easy and My burden is light."*

Here we find Jesus speaking to the crowds. He told them to come to Him and He would give them rest. He then invited them to be yoked with Him and learn of Him. It was common practice in those days to harness two cows together when preparing a field for planting. Usually, one of the animals was stronger and more experienced. They would put another younger cow with the first one. The more experienced animal would train the less experienced one on how to operate in the yoke or harness, under the guidance of the master. Jesus is inviting us to join with Him in relationship and become like Him. Basically, we are called to partner with Him again, as He takes the lead role in our lives. As we do that, we join with Him in His rest which I believe is illustrated in the New Covenant.

REST THROUGH SALVATION

The kind of rest that we have in Christ is based on the work that was done by another, as we mentioned earlier in a quote by A.W. Tozer. Jesus Christ died on the cross, taking the sin of the world on Himself and then overcame the power of sin and death by His resurrection. This allowed us to enter into relationship with Him, the Holy Spirit and the Father and is best explained in both Hebrews 10:16 and Jeremiah 31:33. "But this is the covenant that I will make with the House of Israel after those days, declares the Lord: I will put my law within them and I will write it on their hearts." Jeremiah 31:33. And in Hebrews 10:16 which states, "This is the covenant that I will make with them after those days, declares the Lord: I will put my laws on their hearts, and in their minds I will write them." Then he adds in Hebrews 10:17b "Their sins and their lawless deeds I will remember no more."

The covenant which we now know as the New Covenant is part of how we enter the rest of the Lord. We enter by faith in Christ, as we accept His free gift of salvation. It is not something we can earn but it is a gift, one that writes His ways on our hearts. That is to say that the ways of God, what some might interpret as His rules or laws, become more attractive to us internally. It is like someone changed our insides. 2 Corinthians 5:17, states that the old things have passed away and that all things have become new. Once we receive this gift of salvation, God's ways become appealing to us and the ways that we used to hang onto like partying and self reliance become almost distasteful. In this way, God writes His ways on our hearts, making us feel new.

One definition of a covenant in the Merriam-Webster dictionary is "a written agreement or promise usually under seal between two or more parties especially for the performance of some action."[v] Thus a covenant is an agreement between two parties. A few other words for covenant are contract, commitment and promise.[vi]

Abraham entered into a covenant with God in Genesis 17 when God promised him that he would be the ancestor of many nations. Abraham's descendants kept failing to live up to the standard which God put before them. So God promised a new covenant. One that had been foretold in Genesis 3:15, where God told Eve that her descendants or seed would bruise the serpent's (Satan's) head, making his poison powerless in the lives of men. It was Jesus, Son of God and son of Mary, who came to earth and was without sin who did that very thing. By His death and resurrection, He broke the bondage inflicted on mankind when Satan first deceived Adam and Eve in the Garden of Eden (Genesis 3).

Salvation only comes through accepting Jesus' death and resurrection as His gift to us. Scripture tells us in John 14:6, that this gift only comes through Jesus. " Jesus said to him, *I am the way, the truth, and the life. No one comes to the Father except through Me."*

We rest from any need to perform or earn our salvation or relationship with God as Jesus provided free access to the Father when He died and rose again. When He died on the cross, and spoke His last words, "It is finished." and hung His head and died, it is said that at that time, the curtain to the Holy of Holies in the Jewish Temple was rent from top to bottom (Matthew 27: 50-51a). So God opened the way for us to have access to His presence.

CREATED TO REST

God created us in His own image. He breathed His Spirit in us (Genesis 2:7). And when we accept Jesus as our Savior, the Holy Spirit takes up residence in our hearts. Therefore, part of Him is in us. In one sense, we are made to be like God. We may not have the supernatural powers of God, but our souls long for the things that He longs for. We want to be a part of who He is and share with Him the things that are important to Him. So as He rests, He asks us to join Him in His rest.

ENTER WITH HIM IN HEAVENLY PLACES

The amazing thing is that He invites us to sit with Him in heavenly places, as it says in Ephesians 2:6 "and raised us up with Him and seated us with Him in the Heavenly places in Christ Jesus."

A. W. Tozer states,"By Himself, He purged our sin and sat down on the right hand of God."[vii] His work was finished and He invites us to sit with Him in His state of rest.

Here, we share with Him all that He possesses. We sit with Him and share His place of honor and authority. We cease from our work as we sit in His place in the heavenlies. And it is only because of the finished work of Christ on the cross. This is all because God, the Father, loves us as is further stated in Ephesians 2:4:

"But God, being rich in mercy, because of the great love with which He loved us…"

In a scientific sense, it is as if Jesus is sitting with God in a different dimension which we cannot see. People used to think that there were three or four dimensions.However today ,scientists are speculating that in Superstring theory that there are 10 different dimensions in our universe. Some scientists have even speculated that there are as many as 26 according to Bosonic string theory.[viii] Humans and anything else that have both height, width and length on earth exist in the third dimension. A line on a piece of paper is in the first dimension. Paper is flat, having both height and length. It is in the second dimension. What is in the second dimension cannot see what is on the third dimension. But anyone in the third dimension, which has width, height and length, can see everything in the second dimension clearly. Time is often seen as the fourth dimension. God and Jesus go beyond the dimension of time. God sees things from the beginning of time and also to the end of all time, as if He was presently there. So when we are resting or sitting with Christ in the heavens, it is as if we are sitting in the same dimension He is. However, we need to take this by faith because we can't see into that dimension from our earthly vantage point.

The movie, The Matrix, has some good analogies that might help us see clearer how we can be both seated with Christ and on the earth. In the movie, the good guys, Neo, Morpheus and Trinity, go back into what they had once thought was the real world but was actually a computer generated dream state. Their actual bodies were seated in a chair and hooked up to a machine which put them into "the dream world." The people in the dream world had no idea that they were in a "dream" world. They thought that they were living actual lives. The "awakened ones" like Neo, had been taken out of their sleeping pods where they were used like batteries to fuel the computers which ran the world. They were trying to save the world and defeat the artificial intelligence which had taken over the Earth.

After Paul says to the Ephesians that we are seated in heavenly places with Christ, and therefore at rest with Him, he states that rest does not necessarily mean a cessation of activity. In Ephesians 2:10, Paul states : "For we are His workmanship, created in Christ Jesus for good works, which God prepared beforehand that we should walk in them." Obviously being created to rest doesn't mean we should sleep all day. Rather it is a state of mind. In our rest, we can still work but only in the specific things that Christ has prepared for us to do. This refers back to Matthew 11:28-30, where we are yoked with Christ. As we do this work that He has for us, we again partner with Him and take up that light burden which is in His yoke. I often see my husband do this as He takes time to spend with God through his Bible reading and prayer. God will orangize and orchestrate the tasks, making them easier for him to do.

As we look back at Matthew 11:28, Christ says that He will give us rest, a rest for our souls. This is a rest that starts on the inside. Man is made up of three distinct parts: body, soul and spirit. The soul houses our personality, emotions and will. This is one part of our being that Christ gives rest to after we enter into relationship with Him. That was what God, the Father, always intended for us right from the beginning of time, from when He first thought of creating the universe and everything in it, including us. He wanted relationship. He had Jesus, the angels and all the heavenly beings with Him but God, the Father wanted more. So He created man in His own image, both male and female, so He could relate to them. That man is you and me. God still wants relationship with us, which is why He sent Jesus to Earth {John 3:16).

We see this best illustrated in the beginning of creation after God had created man as Adam and Eve (Genesis 2:7-22). At first, it worked out well. God met with Adam and Eve in the Garden of Eden. They talked and He walked in their midst. But then Satan, the great deceiver, broke up the fellowship they had by enticing them to eat the fruit that would make them "like God," even though they were already made in His image (Genesis 3:1-5). But God had a plan. He made a way to bring man back into relationship with Him. It came through His gift of salvation brought about by our accepting Jesus' death and resurrection which we obtain through faith in Him (Genesis 3:15 and John 3:16). We were created to have relationship with God. He wants to commune with us as He did with Adam and Eve. He desires to walk with us just like the old hymn, "In the Garden" states

"I come to the garden alone, while the dew is still on the roses. And the voice I hear falling on my ear, the Son of God discloses. And He walks with me and He talks with me. And He tells me I am His own. And the joy we share as we tarry there none other has ever known."[ix]

In that relationship we obtain the rest of the Lord. In relationship with Christ, we enter into communion with God without any of our own striving or work. It is a gift, given to us by our Creator. We freely enter into Christ's finished work and into His rest. For myself, I found that this has become more of a reality in the midst of the turmoil which I see on the daily news. Usually, I become angry or upset as I see different things happening in the government or around the world. But as I spend time with Christ in the quiet place, and see myself seated in His rest, I find that I don't feel myself so stirred up inside. The peace of God rests in me as I rest in Him.

ENTER IN

How do we take up the yoke that Jesus offers us in an attempt to find that rest? Hebrews talks about entering the rest of the Lord in chapters 3 and 4. The author of Hebrews illustrates it by referring to the Israelites journey to the Promised Land in chapter three. At the end of chapter three he states that they were not allowed to enter the Promised Land and rest from their wanderings because of their unbelief.

"And to whom did He swear that they would not enter His rest, but to those who were disobedient? So we see that they were unable to enter because of unbelief" Hebrews 3:18-19.

The author goes on to say in Hebrews 4:1 that the promise of God's rest is still available for the people of God: "Therefore, while the promise of entering His rest still stands, let us fear lest any of you should seem to have failed to reach it."

ENTER IN THROUGH FAITH

Hebrews 4:2-3 brings good news. Just as the Israelites could have entered that rest it they had believed, the invitation is still available for us today, if we have faith.

"For good news came to us just as to them, but the message they heard did not benefit them, because they were not united by faith with those

who listened. For we who have believed enter that rest."

We see that it takes faith to enter the rest of the Lord. We have to believe that Jesus is calling us to be yoked with Him and that He has all that we need to enter His rest. Jesus made it abundantly clear that it was possible by His finished work through His death and resurrection for us to enter into His rest. He made a way for all to enter into relationship with God and thus for us to enter into His rest. He was the perfect sacrifice to cover all sin. Thus, no more sacrifice is needed to bring forgiveness between God and man. Jesus finished His work and now sits at the right hand of the Father.

In Deuteronomy 1:19-45, the Israelites were camped out at Kadesh Barnea. They had already come through the wilderness and were poised to enter the Promised Land. God gave them promises along with a command to go in and possess the land. First they sent 12 men in to spy out the land, one from each tribe. They all came back, exclaiming about how fruitful and beautiful the land was. They said, "It is a good land which the Lord our God is giving us"(Deuteronomy 1:25c).

But 10 of the men also spoke anxiously of how large and fierce the inhabitants of the land were. The men complained saying,"Because the Lord hates us, He has brought us out of the land of Egypt to deliver us into the hand of the Amorites, to destroy us"(Deuteronomy 1:27b) and "The people are greater and taller than we, the cities are great and fortified up to heaven; moreover we have seen the sons of the Anakim" (Deuteronomy 1:28b). They didn't have faith that God would keep His word to them in the face of such fierce looking enemies. The Anakim "were a formidable race of giant, warlike people (Deuteronomy 2:10, 21, & 9:2) who occupied the lands of southern Israel near Hebron before the arrival of the Israelites (Joshua 15:13 & 21:11)."[x]

Of the 12 spies, only Caleb and Joshua believed that God would be with them and help them to conquer the people in the land that God had promised them. The Israelites grew fearful, believing the report of the majority of the spies and not on God's promises. Because of that God became angry, and swore an oath that not one of the men of "this evil generation shall see that good land of which I swore to give to your fathers" (Deuteronomy 1:35). Caleb and Joshua were the only ones allowed to enter the land because they had believed that God would faithfully do what He had promised.

Abraham did just the opposite of the disbelieving Israelites. Abraham lived in Ur of the Chaldeans, modern day Iraq. Joshua 24:2 says that Abraham and his father worshiped idols. God asked Abraham to come away from his homeland and follow Him to a new land. Abraham had no experience or reference point from which to base his decision to trust this unknown God. And he had no idea where this unknown God would lead him or whether he

29

would be safe. Yet, he went anyways, trusting God not to lead him astray. Each step of the way, God showed Himself faithful to keep Abraham and his family safe, even when Abraham made mistakes and didn't trust God completely.

For example, Abraham lied to King Abimelech, telling him that Sarai, his wife, was his sister (Genesis 20:2). She was very beautiful. Abraham was afraid that the king would kill him and take Sarai to be his wife. The king then did try to take her as his own wife, but God intervened, speaking to King Abimelech in a dream. God told him not to touch Sarai for she was Abraham's wife (Genesis 20:3). So Abimelech returned her to Abraham, along with sheep, oxen, and servants (Genesis 20:13).

So we see that Abraham was not perfect in how he trusted God either. But God proved Himself faithful to care for and watch over Abraham, even in his failure to trust. God was more interested in the fact that Abraham took the first steps following after Him and pursuing His direction than in making sure that Abraham was obedient 100% of the time.

David is another example of someone who trusted the Lord but wasn't always obedient. In fact, he trusted the Lord so much that he was referred to as "a man after God's own heart" (1 Samuel 13:14, Acts 13:22). Again, he was not perfect in his walk with the Lord. But he continually sought the Lord after he made mistakes, repented and made steps to follow in obedience. In Psalm 51, we see David crying out to God with a repentant heart after he had had an affair with Bathsheba and arranged for her husband's death. Ultimately, we see his walk with God lead him to a place of rest in Psalm 23, the most recognized of all the Psalms. David records his expressions of delight in God's goodness and David's ability to find rest even in the valley of the shadow of death.

We cannot enter into God's rest without trusting the Lord. This is not the easiest thing to do for many people. Most of our experiences in life have led us to do anything but trust others, let alone someone we cannot see. Probably the best way to change that is by getting to know the Lord God Himself. We do that by spending time with Him, and being still before Him. When we are still, His presence can rest on us, giving us peace and opening the door to us resting in Him. We will examine this in the next chapter.

Another way to facilitate entering the Lord's rest and strengthening our faith is by remembering our personal experience of God's faithfulness or our testimony. We strengthen our faith each time, we see our unseen God come through for us in a tangible way. Bible stories from heroes of the faith can strengthen it too but nothing works better than something you can personally remember.

One of my favorite stories which illustrate this happened when I was in college. I had very little money for extras or even for necessities. I had been given a used car by my stepfather my senior year but it needed new tires. I was working a part time job but had no money for unexpected expenses. So I prayed about the need. One Friday shortly after that I was walking across campus on the way to the Student Union. I looked down as I walked and came across a wad of bills on my path. I looked around to see if there was anyone nearby who could have dropped it. Seeing no one, I picked it up. There were five $20 bills. To make certain, that the money was not lost, I turned it into the Student Union lost and found. They told me that in a week, I could return and if no one claimed the money, it would be mine. The next week, I returned and they handed over the $100 to me. I then was able to put the money towards the new tires that I needed. Looking back on this incident, I am reminded how much God loves me and will take care of me. I can rest from fear and anxiety and move in faith in whatever He desires for me to do.

ENTER INTO HIS PRESENCE

In this chapter, we will look at entering God's rest through meditation and through thanksgiving and praise. To experience the rest of the Lord, we need to spend time in His presence. Psalm 37 and Isaiah 26:3 speaks of how we do this. The first part of Psalm 37:7 tells us to, "Be still before the Lord and wait patiently for Him,…"

It is by first being still before the Lord and waiting on Him that we enter into His presence and into His rest. That may seem impossible in the fast paced times that we live in but rest assured it is possible.

It is in the stillness found at the feet of Christ, where we learn to rest in Him. By slowing our senses down and turning off the things that distract us, we are able to hear Him and roll our cares onto His shoulders.

Recently, I started taking at least 15 minutes a day to listen to what God would say to me. Even though it is only 15 minutes, it is not always easy. Distracting thoughts bombard my mind right away, trying to move me from the place of quiet listening. On those days, I often will take a notepad and quickly jot down the "to dos" that are distracting me, telling me what I need to be doing. Other days, the Holy Spirit tells me to worship Him. This is wonderful for I find that it is an excellent way to be led into His presence. To keep myself from running to social media during this time, I will even turn off my phone and other electronic devices which I may be using for a time.

Like Mary, we sit at His feet and allow his spirit to rest in and on us. When Jesus came to Mary's and Martha's home in Bethany, Mary was eager to sit at Jesus' feet and learn from the Master. Jesus said that Mary had chosen the one good thing that was needed (Luke 10:39-42). We should do likewise.

At one point when I was in college, I discovered Isaiah 40:31. I thought it meant that if I got busy serving the Lord in the Christian group, that He would renew my strength. I soon wore myself out with all that I was doing. Then the Lord began to show me that my strength wasn't renewed in the "busy-ness" of serving Him like a waitress. But rather it was by my sitting and waiting for Him to rest upon me, filling me with His presence. As I did that, He revitalized my tired body, enabling me to do more. Our strength of mind and body is renewed as we sit before Him, meditating on His word and presence. Resting in Jesus, therefore, renews our body and also our minds.

Jesus, Himself, would often go to a quiet place to listen to the Father and regain strength. He needed those times to renew Himself and hear the Father's voice more clearly. He told the disciples in Mark

6:31a, "Come with me by yourselves to a quiet place and get some rest."

If Jesus and the disciples needed quiet time before the Father, how much more do we?

ENTER IN THROUGH MEDITATION

We know that we enter by faith. And faith is produced by meditation on God's word (Romans 10:17). So that's a good place to start. Mary was blessed to sit at Jesus' feet and listen to Him teach (Luke 10:39). We don't have His actual physical presence with us but we have His words in the Bible and the Holy Spirit who shows us Jesus and fills us with His presence. Reading or meditating on the word of God slowly and reflecting on it helps us to enter His presence and obtain His rest. By slowly reading a Bible passage over and over again, the truths sink into our minds on a deeper level and bring our subconscious into the presence of God. I highly recommend journaling during this process where you can draw pictures impressed on you from the passage or take notes about the scripture. It may help you stay on track and note your progress as you read the Bible passages over and over again.

In 2013, I traveled to Entebbe, Uganda to an orphanage called Abba House. The main purpose of my visit was to teach the children how to prayer journal. We brought with us composition notebooks and colored pencils for each child from the youngest of 4 years old to the oldest of 17 years old. Before we had left we had talked with some people in the area who did prayer journaling with elementary children. Lelonie Hibbard, a teacher and chaplain for the elementary grades at The Daniel Academy, a Christian school in Kansas City, went over a few of the dynamics of prayer journalling before I left for Africa. In Uganda, I divided the children into two different age groups and then would give them a scripture passage to meditate on. We would read the scripture aloud together as a group, then read it again slowly. Then each of the children would either read it to themselves or even sing the scripture. When they were impressed with something, they would either write or draw a picture about it. I repeated this method about four times during the week with each group. The children loved the entire process, drawing many beautiful pictures and writing words of wisdom which they had gotten from meditating on the scripture.

ENTER IN THROUGH THANKSGIVING AND PRAYER

When we first try to come into the presence of the Lord, we should be thankful. Psalms 100:4 states that we are to enter His gates with thanksgiving. Gates refer to doors or entryways. The Merriam Webster dictionary defines gate in two ways. The first definition refers to it as "an opening in a wall or fence." The second definition refers to it as "a city or castle entrance often with defensive structures (such as towers)."[xi] Before we come into the presence of the Lord, we often feel separated from Him as if by a wall that we cannot see. Jesus broke down that wall so that we can come freely into His presence. Being thankful to Jesus for our salvation is often the first step in our walking with Him in relationship. By telling Him that we are thankful, it is almost like an invitation for Him to come be with us.

Also, Philippians 4:6 says that we should always ask God with thanksgiving. So we thank God for His rest even before we enter it. That prepares the way for us to enter His presence where we can come into His rest.

Entering into the rest of the Lord is also often maintained as we learn to pray without ceasing (1 Thessalonians 5:17). Prayer is simply talking to God. This can be about our day or about the needs of ourselves or others. God likes us to partner with Him. One way to do this is to ask Him for things. By talking to God throughout the day, we are acknowledging that He is with us always. His presence is resting in us even though we don't see Him or feel Him. This by-product of our giving Him our prayer requests is the peace of God which guards our hearts and minds as mentioned in Philippians 4:7.

REST = ABIDING

Another way to look at entering the rest of the Lord is to look at how it relates to our abiding in Christ. Two of the definitions for abiding are "to stay or live somewhere: and "to remain or continue."[xii] Synonyms for abide include words like continue, remain, survive, last, persist, stay and live on.[xiii] When we rest in Christ, we also remain in Him. This is what we are called to do.

Jesus spoke of it in John 15:4-7. He illustrates what it means to abide using an agrarian example of branches abiding in the vine. The branch cannot survive on its own. The sap which feeds the vine is also a part of the branches that are attached to it. If the branch were to be separate from the vine, it would be separated from its life source and thus wither and die. Verse four tells us "abide in Me, and I in you." This goes beyond the concept of partnership and speaks of union with Christ. Jesus states in John 15:5,

"I am the vine, you are the branches. Whoever abides in Me and I in him, he it is that bears much fruit, for apart from Me you can do nothing."

The fruit of the Christian life comes not because we are striving to produce it but because the Spirit of God is connected to us, working in us to produce it. It is much like the sap in the vine which produces life in the branches. The tree does nothing to produce the fruit. It does not strive or toil. We don't hear it say, "I have to produce now." The sap goes through the tree and instinctively knows when to produce the flowers. Bees and birds pollinate them and then fruit grows. Eventually, it ripens and is eaten.

I think of the time in my early walk with the Lord how I struggled to quit smoking. I didn't seem to have the power to quit at the time. One time a person came up to me and told me that I shouldn't be smoking because I was a Christian. I knew that I was struggling but I responded in faith saying, "I know that I am still smoking but I know that I will quit because of Philippians 1:6 which says, *Being confident of this very thing, that He who has begun a good work in you will complete it until the day of Jesus Christ.*" Within two months of that incident, I had quit smoking with no desire to start again. The desire completely left me as I determined in faith that Christ would do the work in me, just as I abide in or dwell in Him.

In the same way, the Spirit of the Lord produces fruit in our lives when we are abiding or in union with Christ. As I stated earlier, life apart from Jesus, who is our life source, is actually no life at all. Rather, it is a form of death, as illustrated in John 15:6.

"If you do not remain in me, you are like a branch that is thrown away and withers, such

branches are picked up, thrown into the fire and burned." (John 15:6 NIV)

As we abide in Christ, we abide in His love. This is also a part of His character. John 15:9-10(NIV) tells us to abide in His love. It also states that if we obey His commands, we will abide in Him. "As the Father has loved me, so have I loved you. Now remain in my love, just as I have kept My Father's commandments and abide in His love." Jesus states that He has kept His Father's commandments and thus abides in His love. Just as the young ox that is yoked with the mature ox learns by example, we also learn by being yoked with Jesus and like Him we abide in the love of God, the Father.

REST = REFUGE

Not only does the rest of the Lord bring us into that abiding which we often think of as union with the Lord, but it also brings us into a place of refuge. When fear tries to buffet me, the first place in scripture that I turn to is Psalm 91

Psalm 91:1-2 says:

"He who dwells in the secret place of the Most High Shall abide under the shadow of the Almighty. I will say of the Lord, 'He is my refuge and my fortress': My God in Him, I will trust."

Here the scriptures talk about abiding with God. To abide is also to dwell. As we dwell in the secret place of the Most High, where we pray and commune with Him, we are also abiding in Him. We come to know Him intimately as He shelters and protects us. Verse one promises that as we rest (dwell,abide) in the secret place of the Most High God we will not be moved. This verse doesn't mean that nothing bad will come into our lives after we enter into relationship or union with the Lord, but it does take the sting out of it for us.

I have often imagined what it must have been like to have been on the boat with Jesus crossing the Sea of Galilee when the storm came up (Matthew 8:23-27). The disciples were agitated and afraid as the boat was tossed on the water. Yet, Jesus slept peacefully.

In their unrest, they woke Jesus who then rebuked them for their lack of faith and commanded the storm to cease. The rest that Jesus had in the boat is what He carried with Him wherever He went. We can learn from Him. When we hit rough patches and storms in our lives our goal is to keep our hearts and minds free from fear, like Jesus did.

A few years ago, many people were plagued with a fear of the new Swine Flu. Doctors and health officials warned that it might sweep the country. I remember some of my friends being afraid and gearing up to combat the ominous flu. Some of my friend's families caught it. They had to wear masks when they went to the pharmacy for medication. Many young adults actually died from the flu strain that year. The niece of one of my friends died. She was only 21 years old. However, I was not afraid. I had felt the nudge of the Holy Spirit to lay hold of the promise found in Psalm 91:9-10, which states:

"Because you have made the LORD, who is my refuge even the Most High, your dwelling place. No evil shall befall you, nor shall any plague come near your dwelling."

Both that year and the years after, not one member of my family got that flu.

Again, it takes faith to enter into that secret place of the Lord. We have to believe that God loves us and that He will take care of us in the middle of life's battles. It also takes obedience. We have to take the necessary steps to obey Him, spend time with Him and seek intimacy with Him. For my life, this means setting time aside daily where I can pray and meditate on the Word of God. Then as I sense the presence of the Lord, usually by a warm sensation inside my chest, I pray silently and sit in the presence of the Lord, letting His presence fill me. Some days this is easier than others. Life has it's challenges with multiple interruptions which try to keep me from spending time with the Lord. I have had to make it a priority, turning off my phone and setting aside that time. Sometimes, I will journal my thoughts as I pray, adding a sidebar on my page for distracting thoughts and reminders of things that I need to do which keep assaulting my mind during prayer. My husband often takes time to go walk in a park. There when he is by himself and with no one nearby, he will talk out loud to the Lord.

David spoke often of God being His refuge. In Psalm 62:1(NIV), David said, "I find my rest in God alone. He is the One who saves me." And then in Psalm 62:2 which says "He only is my rock and my salvation; he is my defense; I shall not be greatly moved," Here David speaks of God being his rock and defense, stating that he would not be moved. David was under attack as he was writing this Psalm. In David Guzik's commentary, he states that Psalm 62 was written during a time of trouble for King David.[xiv] He asserts that "David trusted in God alone for his strength and stability. The description is of a man completely focused upon God for his help, firmly resolved to look nowhere else."[xv] Tradition states that this Psalm was written during the period when his son, Absalom, led a rebellion against him. Although the rebellion came about due to sin in David's own family, he still trusted in God. In 2 Samuel 15 we find the story of how Absalom attacks David. David flees and refuses to attack back. Instead, he waits upon God to intervene.[xvi] In Psalm 62:6, David makes this declaration of faith:

"He only is my rock he is my defense; I shall not be moved, in God is my salvation and my glory, the rock of my strength; and my refuge is in God."

We notice here that God is David's defense and that he will not be moved. David speaks more emphatically, here than in Psalm 62:2. There, he states that he will not be "greatly moved." In verse six, he goes on to say that he will not be moved at all, period. I believe that since he is refusing to move, he has found a place of rest.

The latter part of verse seven states "And my refuge is in God." The Blue Letter Bible app states that the Hebrew word for God is "Elohiym", and the prefix is "ba" which means in God, of God, by God, or through God.[xvii] Ba is a connector word.[xviii] It could be stated that David's refuge is through God.

Let's compare this to the illustration of the vine in John 15:4 where Jesus tells the disciples to "Abide in Me and I in you." Even though this translation of John 15:4 comes from the Greek, I believe it is similar. As the Greek word "en", means "in, of,by, with, or through." The in after abide is "en" and also after I in John 15:4. "Jesus tells His disciples to be in union with Him, to produce fruit."[xix] David is referring to his refuge as a union with God. Even though he is in the middle of a tumultuous time he is finding his rest and peace through the Lord. Nothing is able to shake him from his place of dwelling/abiding.

David also speaks in Psalm 64:1-4 of having no fear when others speak against him.

"Hear my voice, O God, in my meditation; preserve my life from fear of the enemy. Hide me from the secret plots of the wicked, from the rebellion of the workers of iniquity, who sharpen their tongue like a sword, and bend their bows to shoot their arrows--bitter words, that they may shoot in secret at the blameless; Suddenly they shoot at him and do not fear."

God will fight his battles for him. Verse eight states that God will make them stumble over their own tongue. "So He will make them stumble over their own tongue; all who see them shall flee away," (Psalm 64:8). Psalm 64:9 emphasizes the fact that God fights for him again:

"All men shall fear, And declare the work of God; For they shall wisely consider His doing. The righteous shall be glad in the Lord, and trust in Him. And all the upright in heart shall glory."

Verse 10 states that the righteous will be glad in the Lord and trust in Him. Here again, the reference is made to the preposition "in." David is at peace in God. Therefore, he trusts in God and is glad in Him.

In our own daily struggles, we can learn from David's example where he continues to trust that God will fight his battles for him. I have found this to be the case when I have felt that the world is against me. Recently, I had a strange fall in my backyard where my left leg went out from underneath me as I went from my patio door to the landing step outside. I fell backwards and to the left, off my landing onto the little white patio rocks to the side of the concrete landing steps, barely missing the faucet spigot and the side of the house with my head. The little rocks somehow displaced my weight, cushioning my fall. I didn't hurt my head nor my back. I only sustained a bruise on my right front shin as my leg caught a hold of a potted plant on my way down. Because of my fall, my husband decided that I shouldn't go on a trip that I was looking forward to. For the next week, I had to keep my foot up, easing the swelling in my right shin. I felt that the world was against me. The Lord spoke to my heart, telling me to be still and let Him fight my invisible enemies. I was reminded of Psalm 46:10:

"Be still, and know that I am God; I will be exalted among the nations, I will be exalted in the earth!"

And also in Psalm 46: 1-2

"God is our refuge and strength, a very present help in trouble. Therefore we will not fear, Even though the earth be removed, and though the mountains be carried into the midst of the sea;"

Exodus 14:13-14 also speaks of God fighting for the Israelites as they remained still,

"And Moses said to the people, Do not be afraid. stand still, and see the salvation of the Lord, which He will accomplish for you today. For the Egyptians whom you see today, you shall see again no more forever. The Lord will fight for you, and you shall hold your peace."

I am also reminded of these verses, when I watch the national news. Nothing can deter me from the rest of the Lord more than all the emotional hype I get when I watch it. I have to remind myself daily of where I am positioned with Christ and that He is over the earth. He will bring forth His Justice. These thoughts clear my mind from the swirling news and allow His peace to reign in my heart. Indeed, the rest of the Lord is my refuge from the headlines of today which stir me up and get me agitated.

BENEFITS OF REST

As we discussed in previous chapters, there are
several by-products of being at rest in the Lord.
When we are at rest, we are at peace. Our minds are
calm and we find rest for our soul. Secondly, when
we are at rest, whether physically or spiritually, we
are rejuvenated. By spending time at the feet of
Jesus, meditating on the Word of God and being
intimate with Him, we find new sources of strength
which God gives to us. But there are other benefits
of entering into rest. For instance, we have joy.

Have you ever noticed that when you worship God,
a sense of joy or happiness overtakes you?
Worshiping God and/or being thankful produces
feelings of joy. One of the fruits of the Spirit is joy
(Galatians 5:22). The fruits of the Spirit are
produced when we abide in Him. We can look at
the early Christians who, even when they were
persecuted and their lives were threatened, would
sing praises to God and be joyful.

A good example is found in Acts 16:16-26 where
Paul and Silas were imprisoned.

*"But at midnight Paul and Silas were praying
and singing hymns to God, and the prisoners
were listening to them. Suddenly there was a
great earthquake, so that the foundations of the
prison were shaken; and immediately all the*

doors were opened and everyone's chains were loosed" (Acts 16:25-26).

Here we see that as they trusted and rested in God, it allowed praise to fill them, and He fought for them. Not only do Paul and Silas remain peaceful in the midst of their trial, but the joy which bubbled up inside of them released an act of God and they were freed from their chains.

I often think of how the fruit of the spirit produced in our lives is like that of fruit produced on a fruit tree. The tree does not plan or work to produce fruit. It doesn't decide one day to grow an apple. It is programmed into the DNA of the apple tree to produce apples. So when we abide and rest in Christ, our spiritual DNA becomes changed to Christ's DNA, where we become like Him and naturally produce the fruit of the Spirit. Along this track, 2 Corinthians 3:18 states, "But we all, with unveiled face, beholding as in a mirror the glory of the Lord, are being transformed into the same image from glory to glory, just as by the Spirit of the Lord."

Graham Cooke has stated that our rest in God is our weapon.[xx] In the You Tube video referenced in the footnote, Graham Cooke tells the story of how this came to him in 1981 when he was reading a spy novel by Robert Ludlin out on his back patio. Graham came to a part where the character talks about sleep being his weapon. Graham knew that is what the book actually said, but the words in his head said, "Rest was his weapon." That led to him looking up the scripture passage in Matthew 11:28-30, where Jesus invites us to be yoked with Him and find rest.

My family's friend, Jenny Patten, exuded joy, even in the face of pain and adversity. She always had a joyful attitude. She didn't talk about her trials. She smiled through her hardships. I remember her standing by her house, talking to my grandmother and helping people in the neighborhood. She hosted missionaries from American Missionary Fellowship who came each summer to teach a rural Vacation Bible School in the local Grange building. She worked cheerfully and tirelessly even though she suffered from a blood disorder which left her weak. I learned this from my mother who often assisted Aunt Jenny.

We come into rest by faith and thankfulness which in itself produces more praise, joy and peace. That peace shines through our character, showing others the image of Christ in our lives, thus transforming our lives from glory to glory as stated in 2 Corinthians 2:18. As we sit in His presence, and thus in His rest, we are changed into the very image of Christ.

THE BENEFIT OF ABUNDANT LIFE

Another benefit of resting in Christ is that it makes life flourish. By waiting in the presence of Christ and meditating on His scriptures we flourish and prosper in our lives. Psalm 1:2-3 says,

"But his delight is in the law of the Lord; and in His law, he meditates day and night; He shall be like a tree planted by the rivers of water, that brings forth its fruit in its season. And whatsoever he does shall prosper."

We also find this in John 10:10, "The thief does not come except to steal, and to kill, and to destroy. I have come that they may have life, and that they may have it more abundantly." Here we see how God loves to partner with us, blessing us in the place of rest as He came to give us abundant life.

Rest Leads to Courage and Confidence

Also, when we are at rest, there is an absence of fear in the midst of turbulent situations. Jesus is our best example of this. He carried His rest with Him in the storms of life. He didn't become agitated when bad things happened. He trusted in His Heavenly Father, talking with Him often in the midst of life. We see this as He talked with God through the night in the Garden of Gethsemane before He was arrested (Mark 14:32-50). Jesus did experience despair as evidenced in Luke 44: 22-43 when He sweat drops of blood, but He did not fear.

This new found courage leads us to work from a place of confidence in our relationship with Christ as we are able to come before the throne of grace boldly (Hebrews 4:16).

CONCLUSION

We should all endeavor to enter into the rest of the Lord. In fact, in Hebrews 4:1, the scripture goes as far as to say that we should fear if we fall short of entering into His rest.

We enter His rest by faith. We obtain faith by meditating on the Word and being in the presence of God. Entering His rest is an act of obedience. We obey God by having faith in Christ and trusting in Him. This pleases God. It leads us developing an intimate relationship with Him and also experiencing His pleasure over us at the same time.

We partner with Jesus in rest by being yoked with Him. A good example of this is shown in John 15. By looking at the vine and the branches, we see a perfect illustration of resting in Christ. The branch has no life apart from the vine and does not worry about the fruit that it produces. Psalm 1:3 also illustrates this by referring to the tree by the rivers of water; our lives are like the tree when we meditate on the scriptures, which produces fruit in its season

"He shall be like a tree, planted by the rivers of water, that brings forth its fruit in its season, whose leaf also shall not wither; and whatever he does shall prosper."

We rest in the Lord when we are seated with Him in the heavenlies, as referenced in Ephesians 2:6. We do not strive to sit, but when we are seated we are at rest. Thus again, we enter by faith, as we can't see the chair in which we are seated.

The beauty of resting in the Lord is not only that it produces spiritual fruit in our lives, but that it produces joy and peace. The fruit of the Spirit grows naturally or rather supernaturally, as we rest in Him. His character also grows in our lives as we rest in Him. The rest of the Lord is also the safest place we can be. We are at peace and will not be shaken when difficult times come our way. He becomes our refuge and our hiding place. Just as I rested on the raft while the tide was going out, we rest in Christ, finding peace and joy for our souls. We can enter in and know that we won't be shaken in the midst of turmoil and conflict as referenced in Psalm 62:6-7.

By meditating on the Word and spending time in prayer and in the presence of God, we maintain the rest of the Lord in our lives. We are renewed in body and mind as we rest in Him. He indeed restores our souls. Waiting on Him in the quiet place, causes us to rise like eagles and run and not grow weary (Isaiah 40:31).

It is God's desire to allow us to enter His rest as we turn to Him in faith. He wants us to experience all His fullness and have that abundant life which He promised us in John 10:10. It is not only His desire but His delight to work that within us. He loves to partner with us in that way.

However it doesn't mean that we should sit and do nothing. Ephesians 2:10 says:

"For we are His workmanship, created in Christ Jesus for good works, which God prepared beforehand that we should walk in them."

So God has prepared things for us to do with Him before the beginning of time. These are good works that will glorify Him. The last part of verse 10 is very significant, "that we should walk in them."

As we are at rest or in union with Him, we walk in what God has prepared for us to do. It is a daily step by step process of walking with Him in His rest that leads us into all the things which He has for us. These things go from a fruit filled life, to abundance, to restoration, to being hidden in Him, to resting in His refuge. Indeed God gives good gifts to His children who turn to Him in faith and obedience. He is a good Father who loves to give good gifts. Our life in Christ is like a big room with a narrow opening or gate. I am reminded of the time machine on the long running PBS show, Doctor Who. From the outside, the time machine looks like a narrow British police box. But once you enter the box, it opens up to a time machine or space ship with lots of room. We enter through faith in Christ. But once we enter, it opens up to a whole new land, one that is flowing with symbolic milk and honey, just as He had promised the Israelites when they came into the

Promised Land (Exodus 13:5, Leviticus 20:24). We can know the fullness of God, only as we enter His rest. It is the goodness of God that allows us to have all of it. It is a free gift through Christ's death and resurrection, not something we can work at or earn in our own efforts. It is God who works the desire in us for it and who draws us to Himself in his loving kindness.

> *"The Lord has appeared of old to me, saying: 'Yes, I have loved you with an everlasting love; Therefore with loving kindness, I have drawn you.'"*

> *(Jeremiah 31:3)*

This in itself creates praise to God in our spirit man and again helps us to maintain the rest of the Lord in our soul. So once we get started in this cycle, it replicates itself, producing praise and rest in Him who is our source, giving glory to the Father through the Son. We give praise to the one who created us for His good pleasure, so that we can share in His rest for now and for all eternity.

My hope in writing this book is that you can apply some of these suggestions and learn how to enter into the rest of the Lord. I hope that next week you find yourself resting in the Lord more than this week, and so also next month, and next year. My prayer for you is that the Lord would bless you as you seek to enter into His rest. May He shower you with all His benefits, so that you ultimately become more like Him.

About the Author

Elizabeth Zacharias lives in Missouri with her husband of 24 years and her 2 young adult daughters. She graduated from the University of Maine at Orono with a degree in Social Work. Originally from Maine, she has lived in Missouri for close to 20 years, homeschooling her daughters.

She is passionate about her pursuit of God, prayer, missions and her creative endeavors. She loves exploring the outdoors, foreign cuisines, writing and chocolate. She longs to see others come into an intimate relationship with Christ and also into their own creative and spiritual potentials which she believes God designed for them from the beginning of time.

To learn more about Elizabeth, visit
createdtorest.com

REFERENCES

[i] "Rest" *Merriam-Webster.com* 2018. https://www.merriam-webster.com (June 18,2018)

[ii] "Enter Into the Rest of Jesus" *Sermon Index.net* 2018. https://www.sermonindex.net/modules/mydownloads/visit.php?lid=2341 (August 28, 2018)

[iii] "Sabbath".*Bible Study Tools.com.* June 2018. www.https://biblestudytools.com (June 2018)

[iv] Sharonne Cohen, "What is an Eruv?" Nov. 2018 https://www.myjewishlearning.com.cdn.ampproject.org (November 2018)

[v] "covenant" *Merriam-Webster.com.* 2018. https://www.merriam-webster.com (August 28,2018)

[vi] "covenant" synonyms *Merriam-Webster.com.* 2018https://www.merriam-webster.com (August 28, 2018)

[vii] "Enter Into the Rest of Jesus" *Sermon Index.net* 2018. https://www.sermonindex.net/modules/mydownloads/visit.php?lid=2341 (August 28,2018)

[viii] Subhash Chandra Sawhney, "What are the 26 dimensions?" November 2018 https://www.quora.com/Whatarethetwentysixdimen

sions   (Oct. 28, 2017)

ix C. Austin Miles, "In The Garden." 1912. Reprint by *God Tube.com* 2018. www.https://godtube.com. (June 18, 2018)

x "Who were the Anakim?" *Got Questions.org* Retrieved   [June   18,   2018],   from https://www.gotquestions.org./Anakim

xi   "Gate"   *Merriam-Webster.com*   2018. www.https://merriam-webster.com   (October   16, 2018)

xii "Abide" *Merriam-Webster.com June 18,2018 www.https://merriam-webster.com. (June 18, 2018)*

xiii "Abide" synonyms *Merriam-Webster.com.* June 18, 2018 www.https://merriam-webster.com. (June 18, 2018)

xiv David Guzik, *Enduring Word Commentary.*June 2018.   www.https://enduringword.com   (December 21, 2015)

xv Ibid

xvi Ibid

xvii *Blue Letter Bible Hebrew Interlinear for Androids*(2018)   www.https://blueletterbible.org. [Mobile   application   software]   Retrieved   from www.http ://googleplay.com

xviii Ibid

[xix] *Blue Letter Bible Greek Lexicon for Androids* (2018) www.http://blueletterbible.org. [Mobile application software] Retrieved from www.http://googleplay.com

[xx] Graham Cooke "The Practise of Rest" *Brilliant Book House.* August 28, 2018 YouTube video, 9:24 Uploaded February 18, 2011 www.https://m.youtube.com/watch

61685062R00040

Made in the USA
Columbia, SC
25 June 2019